Barbara,

    May my book be a reminder of God's love for you.

    Avar James

Following His Lead

Poems That Lift Your Spirit

AVAR H. JAMES

Copyright © 2017 Avar H. James.

All rights reserved. No part of this book may be used or reproduced by any means, graphic, electronic, or mechanical, including photocopying, recording, taping or by any information storage retrieval system without the written permission of the author except in the case of brief quotations embodied in critical articles and reviews.

WestBow Press books may be ordered through booksellers or by contacting:

WestBow Press
A Division of Thomas Nelson & Zondervan
1663 Liberty Drive
Bloomington, IN 47403
www.westbowpress.com
1 (866) 928-1240

Because of the dynamic nature of the Internet, any web addresses or links contained in this book may have changed since publication and may no longer be valid. The views expressed in this work are solely those of the author and do not necessarily reflect the views of the publisher, and the publisher hereby disclaims any responsibility for them.

Any people depicted in stock imagery provided by Thinkstock are models, and such images are being used for illustrative purposes only.
Certain stock imagery © Thinkstock.

THE HOLY BIBLE, NEW INTERNATIONAL VERSION®, NIV® Copyright © 1973, 1978, 1984, 2011 by Biblica, Inc.® Used by permission. All rights reserved worldwide.

Scripture quotations marked (NLT) are taken from the Holy Bible, New Living Translation, copyright © 1996, 2004, 2007 by Tyndale House Foundation. Used by permission of Tyndale House Publishers, Inc., Carol Stream, Illinois 60188. All rights reserved.

Scripture taken from the King James Version of the Bible.

Scripture taken from the Holy Bible: International Standard Version®.
Copyright © 1996-forever by The ISV Foundation. ALL RIGHTS RESERVED INTERNATIONALLY. Used by permission.

[Scripture quotations are] from the Revised Standard Version of the Bible, copyright © 1946, 1952, and 1971 the Division of Christian Education of the National Council of the Churches of Christ in the United States of America. Used by permission. All rights reserved.

Scripture taken from the New King James Version®. Copyright © 1982 by Thomas Nelson. Used by permission. All rights reserved.

ISBN: 978-1-5127-9491-5 (sc)
ISBN: 978-1-5127-9493-9 (hc)
ISBN: 978-1-5127-9492-2 (e)

Library of Congress Control Number: 2017910400

Print information available on the last page.

WestBow Press rev. date: 7/6/2017

In memory of my father, Leon Hurd, Sr., and my grandmother, Avar Pipkin, and in honor of my mother, Doris Hurd, all of whom are my role models.

To my sister, Mildred, who is my most avid cheerleader.

To my husband, Bill, who is my support.

To my sons, Will and Chris, and my daughter, Ashley, who are my gifts.

To my grandchildren, Ashton, Gabi, Camille, and Brooklyn, who are my delight.

Almighty God, Lord and Savior, has done much for me. He has expressed His love for me, and He has blessed my life in many ways:

He protects me.

He comforts me.

He is my help, my friend, my strength.

He provides for me on a daily basis.

He forgives me.

He has saved me and has given me eternal life.

I worship and adore Him.

He is worthy of all the praise and honor.

Introduction

I consider this book of poems a unique opportunity that God has placed before me. Hence, I am *Following His Lead*. Prior to writing this book, I had written just a few poems. Daily devotionals, dreams, observations, and memories have all been the inspirations and catalysts for my writing. My sister Mildred was amazed at how quickly I could write them. It is from her prodding and the encouragement of others that I decided to publish this book. It is at this point in my life that is the best time and the best place to write. My life experiences are the basis for many poems. I value the talent that God has given me and the willingness to share with readers. The Lord has abundantly blessed me all of my life. It is my desire that your life will be enriched and you will be lifted, encouraged, and reminded of God's love for you as you read. It is my hope that you enjoy reading my poems as much as I enjoyed writing them.

Contents

Discipline

Call Ahead	1
Cross-Training	2
Enjoy the Ride	4
Fix My Mess	5
Grow in Grace	7
Know-How and Know-When	8
The Musts	10
Waiting on God	11
What Now, Lord?	13

Forgiveness

Forgiveness	17
Let It Go	18
White-Out	19

God

All Things	23
Be Blessed	24
The Comforter	25
God's Plan	26
God's Power	27
The Good News	28
He Knows Me	29
The Indwelling	30
Inseparable	32
The Light	33
A Mother's Love	34
His Presence and Power	35

The Resurrection 37
The Riches of God 39
The True Rectifier 40
The Sanctuary 41
His Time 42

God's Word

The Bible 45
Newness 47
Power of the Word 48

Life's Trials

A Blessed "No" 51
As Is 52
Be Encouraged 53
Choices 54
Hope 55
Hurry up and Wait 57
I Phone a Friend 59
Recall 60
We Need the Light 61

Obedience

Different Soils 65
Following His Lead 67
Good Works 68
Integrity 69
Power, Love, and Self-Discipline 70
Serving 71
Sow a Seed 72
Sow and Reap 74

Step up to the Plate 75
Teach the Children 76

Peace

Peace 81
Peace Only Comes 82
Sweet Peace. 83

People in the Bible

Apostle Paul 87
Fearless Zephaniah 89
Joseph and His Brothers 91
Joseph and Mary Flee to Egypt 92
King David. 94
King Solomon 96
Mrs. Job 98
Peter's Focus 99
The Prodigal Son 101
The Rich Young Ruler 103
The Servant Who Lacked 104
The Woman With Healing Faith 105

Praise

Christmas 1981 109
Gift of Faith 111
God's Got My Back. 112
I Saw Daddy 113
P is for Praise. 114
Treasured. 116
What More Can I Do? 117

Prayer

Bow the Knee 121
Meeting Him 122
My Alone Time 123
Pray 124
Pray to God 125
Watch and Pray 126

Purpose

Before and After 129
Get It 130
Spiritual Maturity 131
Yet to Come 132

Temptations

The Devil 137
Lay Them Aside 138
On Guard 139
Seasons of Attack 140
Seeking Snails 141
Side Step of Deception 142
Sin 143
Weeds 144

Discipline

Call Ahead

Have you made reservations?
Have you called ahead?
Have you thought about the afterlife,
Or are you too afraid?

Make preparations
For heaven or for hell.
What is your status with the Savior?
Only you can tell.

Get ready for the end time.
No one knows when it will be.
Get your house in order
If His face you desire to see.

Live each day with no regrets,
As though it were your last.
Try to make a difference
When your life has passed.

Call ahead.
Reserve your spot.
Prep for where you're going.
Whether you are ready or not,
That day is surely coming.

Cross-Training

Cross-country training is a sport
For individuals and teams
To run miles in open air or natural extremes.
You run against competitors and Mother Nature too,
On asphalt, gravel, dirt, and mud,
Over hill, up, down, and through.

Footing, elevation, and direction
You work to perfect.
Stride, pace, and a focused mind
You interject.

Those disciplined cross runners
Train and learn to endure.
They work hard, exert the effort,
And from those workouts, they grow sure.

However, there's a different cross-training,
Yet it's very much the same.
It's one where you come to know the Savior
Who died on the cross.
For our sins, He took the blame.

You cross-train by reading His book
To understand what you are to do.
You train for the battle to know how to win.
You become an obedient Christian and try not to sin.

Your footing, elevation, and direction
You work to perfect.
Stride, pace, and a focused mind
You interject.

Follow the cross in your training.
You will become spiritually fit,
Ready for any competition,
As blessings from God you will certainly get.

Enjoy the Ride

As you begin each day,
Place God and His Son
Where they belong:

In your head,
In your prayers,
In your heart,
And on your tongue.

Let God be your companion,
And let Him be your guide.
You'll be prepared for the journey.
You'll enjoy the ride.

Fix My Mess

The first thing I say
When I'm in distress,
"Lord, please help me
And fix my mess."

This is especially true
When I've done it my way,
Disregarding Your leading,
Which I did not obey.

My decision, though rushed,
Seemed right at the time.
It would come together,
And things would work out fine.

I ignored the nudging,
As I had done before,
Hoping it would be different,
And You'd open the door.

I don't know how long
It is going to take
For me to realize
That You make no mistakes.

It is so distrusting
And thoughtless of me
To disregard Your will,
You, who created me.

You know all about me.
You know what's best.
When I'm not trusting You,
I'm settling for much less.

But You're not a God
Who'd say, "I told you so."
No, You are the only One
Who loves me even more.

You are a compassionate and merciful God.
You are sovereign, all-knowing, even my heart.
I pray to You for Your continuous lead.
I must always follow; that is my part.

Grow in Grace

Life is like a book we read.
Day by day, page by page we proceed.
Just as we read and turn the page,
We grow and advance to the next stage.

Infants, tots, teens, young adult years,
Middle age, advancing to senior years;
As we continue through the book,
Things take on a different look.

Eyesight dims, and hair turns gray.
Our steps get shorter, and we sway.
Our bones ache, and muscles get sore
With pain we never felt before.

There are some advantages in growing old.
If you're in Christ, more wisdom you hold.
An appreciation of life you never had
Because good days outnumber the bad.

Just as we complete reading the book,
We are now more informed.
As we grow in grace,
Our lives have been transformed.

We live each day with gratitude and praise
That God will strengthen our days.
And even when our health fails,
We know His will will prevail.

Know-How and Know-When

Know-how and know-when
Are two important gifts
Instilled by the Holy Spirit
On what we would speak.

When we see a need
That we can fill,
It is wise to know
How and when to appeal.

Know-how is
Knowing exactly what to say.
In any situation,
There is a right way.

Know-when is
Knowing exactly when to say
And when to remain silent
If it is care you want to convey.

Be open and receptive
To what He has to say,
For His words to be clear
As you awaken to pray.

His words of wisdom
You cannot possibly know
Until you've listened to Christ
And allowed the Spirit to flow.

Then echo His words
Into the heart of the weary.
Voiced at the right time and in the right way,
It brings hope and helps to fill a need sincerely.

The Musts

There are things
In each believer's life
That supersede
And surpass all others.

Those are the musts,
The things we have to do,
If to our Lord and Savior
We want to remain true.

We must
Put Him first,
Read His Word,
Obey His commands,
Love our neighbor,
Tell about His love,
Be a light of hope,
Allow Him to use us,
And work each day as unto the Lord.

Waiting on God

Patience is waiting on God.
    Patience means I don't worry or fret
    Because my prayers haven't been answered yet.
    Patience is working and praying,
    Knowing that God might be delaying.

Time is waiting on God.
    Time is knowing that His time
    Is not ever the same as mine.
    It's knowing that His time is perfect and exact
    And knowing mine is nothing like that.

Silence is waiting on God.
    Silence is being spiritually still
    As God's purposes are fulfilled
    And being confident that I am at rest.
    God wants for me His very best.

Trust is waiting on God.
    Trust is believing what I can't see
    And hoping for what I expect to be.
    Trust is being assured that God keeps His Word,
    Even if my ears have not heard.

Patience, time, silence, and trust—
    Each of these is a must.
    For God's will and way I behold
    The glorious blessings He will unfold.

All nature, all growth, all peace, everything that flowers and is beautiful to the world depends on patience, requires time, silence, trust.
    —Herman Hesse

What Now, Lord?

You've accepted Jesus Christ
As your personal Lord and Savior.
It was your best decision
To secure eternal life favor.

"What now, Lord?"
You might ask,
As you seek to do His will
For your new life.

God has things
He wants you to do,
And there are places
He wants you to go.

Pray, study His Word,
Be watchful for His signs,
Associate with fellow believers
Who have like minds.

Listen to the inner voice
That speaks to you.
That's the Holy Spirit,
Who will guide you through.

Trust God
With every detail of your life.
He will strengthen you
With His unfailing love.

Watch, listen, and follow.
Is your challenge, then,
What God calls you to do,
He enables you to attend.

Forgiveness

Forgiveness

Rejection, abuse, or misunderstanding
Could very well be the cause
Of the hurt and resentment you hold
That could put your life on pause.

Seventy times seven,
Or as many as it takes,
Is what God commands
To forgive others' mistakes.

Bitterness, anger, and regret
Are not part of the plan.
They all can be removed
By forgiving your fellow human.

Release the past,
Which cannot be changed.
A willingness to forgive
Is what can be arranged.

Remember God's grace.
Remain aware of His love.
Recall the number of times
You've been forgiven from above.

Forgiveness can empower.
Burdens of negativity will cease.
Barriers are removed.
When you forgive and let go,
You will be at peace.

Let It Go

To forgive is a command
Given to us by God.
Letting go of guilt and hurt
He knew would be hard.

Unforgiveness is a heavy weight
That easily pulls you down.
Unchain it quickly;
You'll be better all around.

Unforgiveness has power;
It's a destructive, insidious force.
It frustrates your efforts;
It takes you off course.

Forgiveness is needed
By every woman and man.
It lifts burdens of the past,
And peace will come at last.

Forgiveness gives you power.
It puts you in control.
When you forgive and forget,
You are the better soul.

You will be at peace
When God's command you obey.
Forgiving is His will.
Forgiving is His way.

White-Out

Once written in ink,
We cannot erase.
White-Out was created
To cover our mistakes.

Wouldn't it be great
If we could White-Out
The mistakes we made
That caused much guilt and doubt?

Actually, there is a White-Out.
Jesus is His name.
He knows all our sins
And loves us just the same.

Humbly seek His face;
Repent and be at peace.
He erases our mistakes;
Our guilt can then cease.

He releases all our guilt.
He forgets and He forgives.
Go to Him in earnest;
Our forgiveness is His.

White-Out lets us cover up,
So then we can rewrite.
We have another chance
To this time get it right.

God

All Things

Life seems carefree and oh so good
When things go as we think they should.
But this journey that is called life
Includes disappointments and times of strife.
Things go awry of a well-made plan,
Making it difficult to understand.
But as Christians, we should not fret,
For God has never failed us yet.
He does not want us to be helpless
For His power works best in our weaknesses.

What is found in Romans 8:28
Helps us better understand our fate.
When problems arise and cause much pain,
God can turn a burden to gain.
And the woe that is distressing,
God can turn into a blessing.
There's no room for doubt or criticism;
Only a basis for lifelong optimism.
Satan wants to kill, steal, and destroy,
But God gives you an abundant life to enjoy.

God directs all things for you and me.
That's not a goal but His guarantee.
He works things out for the good
As only a sovereign God could.
Know that God loves us, and He's in control.
To obey and trust Him is our role.
We serve a God who knows what is best.
Pray and praise Him; He'll do the rest.
On our pathways, every moment of each day,
Keep trusting, and let God have His way.

Be Blessed

Perhaps you've seen a sign or heard someone say,
"Be blessed," "God bless," or "Have a blessed day."
You see it, hear it, and then you ponder;
What does it mean, you might wonder.

It means wherever you go or whatever you do,
God's presence is wanted for you,
Whether you are in need or even if not,
Whether you're freezing cold or if you are hot.

Whether your life is going quite well
Or it's so bad, you would not want to tell,
Whether you're sick and in much pain,
Or if the sun is shining or if there is rain.

Whether your soul is in the valley deep
Or up high on a mountain peak,
If you are a believer, God is your friend.
It doesn't matter what situation you're in.

God is with you, and He cares.
Continue to speak to Him in your prayers.
God will show His children favor.
His grace, mercy, and new life you'll savor.

God promised to never leave you alone,
So tell your fears to be gone.
If someone tells you to have a blessed day,
Thank them—and God—and be on your way.

The Comforter

I am not thinking of the comforter on my bed
Or a down-filled quilt or a fluffy bedspread.

I am thinking of the One who comforts me
When sorrow and pain is what I see.

He promises not to leave me so that I am not alone.
He helps me to endure until my weaknesses grow strong.

God is indeed my Comforter.
He keeps me
Warm,
Protected,
And
Secure.

God's Plan

God's plan is what He wants:
A loving relationship with us.
He wants our whole-hearted obedience,
Love, and trust.

We as a people
Will not do right.
We bring much displeasure
To His sight.

If we would obey,
There's nothing He would not do.
He would truly bless us
Through and through.

God has not wavered.
He never will.
We make mistakes,
But He loves us still.

He's waiting on us.
He's giving us time.
But we run, resist, and forget,
Thinking it's not the end of the line.

We must repent
And seek His face.
He forgives with open arms,
Waiting with love and grace.

God's Power

Power from God is manifested as

Help in times of trouble.
He'll be there on the double.

Direction in times of confusion.
His way results in the solution.

Hope in times of disaster.
Look no further than the Master.

Faith in times of fear.
His voice you need and you will hear.

Strength in times of weakness.
His power becomes your fullness.

Comfort in times of affliction.
His love can soothe any condition.

Consolation in times of grief.
His grace supplies wanted relief.

Rest in times of sorrow.
His mercy extends through tomorrow.

The power of God, at His command,
Is given to us, in our hands.

The Good News

The gospel is the good news
That we are told to share
With those who do not know Christ,
So they become aware.

They come to know the reason
Why Christ died for them,
Then it's a matter of repentance
To begin their walk with Him.

Accept Christ in your heart.
Be baptized in the faith.
Begin the transformed life,
Where challenges will await.

And learn his Holy Word
With the promises it provides.
He will make the journey with you,
And it will be worthwhile.

Then you too will pass it on,
The difference this blessed life makes.
Becoming a believer
Is really all it takes.

He Knows Me

God knows everything about me:
My ins and outs, my ups and downs.
He knows what causes me sadness.
He knows what brings me gladness.

When I make plans from the start,
Though unfinished, He knows my heart.
He knows when I need a friend.
He knows when I'm the friend to send.

God knows when I'm scared and stumble.
He knows doubt causes me to fumble.
He even knows the times I fell.
He knows what I'm ashamed to tell.

Even when what I've done
Was not always my best,
It is so amazing:
God loves me, nonetheless.

I know Him too,
And one day must give my account.
From nothing and nowhere can I hide;
Heaven is where I plan to reside.

The Indwelling

Is the Holy Spirit
Comfortable with me?
Each day, is He at peace,
Seeing what I see?

Have I made Him welcome
Or is He ill at ease?
Does it make Him shudder
When I do as I please?

When I mess up big time
And have my selfish thoughts,
Has Satan won again,
When he and I have fought?

Or is the Spirit grieved
When others I neglect?
I miss a chance to help
But feel no real regret.

Is He pleased with me
When he knows my heart,
When I don't follow through
Or claim my part?

I sure hope that I
Have not grieved Him in any way.
I've been so terribly busy
That I took no time to pray.

What good does it do me
For the Holy Spirit to dwell,
If there is no difference in my life
That anyone can tell?

The Holy Spirit has filled me
But I have yet to give control.
It is only when I concede it
That my growth will unfold.

Inseparable

We can never be separated
From the love of God.
We're all in the family
Of which we have become a part.

We will always have His love.
We will always be protected.
We know that we are covered
For whatever is unexpected.

The qualities of our lives
And the direction of our days
Are directly impacted
By His love, which will amaze.

Never will we have to worry.
Never will we have to fear.
We know our Heavenly Father
Is with us, right now, right here.

Never will we get lost.
Never will we lose heart.
We can never be separated
From God's love, there at the start.

The Light

We cover up when we disobey,
Not forthcoming, knowing it's not God's way.

We have the urge to hide misdeeds:
Our inherited nature from Adam and Eve.

But there is another way that's right,
As believers who are exposed to the light.

It's not a life totally free of sinning
But one where sin is no longer winning.

Our sins we longer have to hide.
We bring them to God, where forgiveness abides.

We work through ways to avoid temptation,
Taking God up on his invitation.

The light of Jesus will help you heal
Because God's strength and power are real.

A Mother's Love

God knew from the very start
A mother needed a special heart.
A mother's love is so very dear,
So warm, so comforting, and so sincere.
For her children she will adore.
She seems to love so much more.
No matter what the place in life,
A mother's love will always suffice.
Her love tends to overflow,
As she watches her children grow.
She has a special kind of love,
Given only by the Father above.
Thank You, God, for our mothers
Because their love is like no other.

His Presence and Power

His presence and power
Are all you need.
In any and every task,
You will succeed.

When God is present,
And He is, upon request,
The job will get done
In a way you could not guess.

Just like Nehemiah,
In completing the wall,
His enemies tried with all their might
To frustrate his plans, to discourage them all.

Enemies will discourage you,
For you're considered a threat.
But the power of God, they don't know,
Has not failed anyone yet.

When we encounter opposition,
And most certainly we will,
Be encouraged as a disciple of Christ
For God's way to be fulfilled.

His presence and power,
What a difference they make,
In whatever endeavor
You strive to undertake.

All things are possible,
For those who believe.
What is impossible for enemies and men,
God's presence and power can achieve.

The Resurrection

The proof is in the resurrection.
He did what He said that He would do.
He was committed to become the Savior,
For He spoke only what was true.

The proof is in the resurrection.
God began with the end in mind.
He knew Judas, Herod, Pilate, and the Jews
Would do what they did; He even knew what time.

The proof is in the resurrection.
He did what no other could ever do.
He suffered, He bled, and He died,
But He rose for me and you.

The proof is in the resurrection.
Pilate's guards stood by the grave for three days.
The tomb was sealed and secured;
All was futile, for His body did not stay.

The proof is in the resurrection.
We remember on Easter Day.
We honor, praise, and glorify Him,
For His Father He did obey.

The proof is in the resurrection.
The holy Creator of the universe
Took up the likeness of sinful man,
Knowing full well that He'd be crucified
By His own sinful men.

Yes, the proof is in the resurrection,
And I'm so glad that it is.
It shows the depth of His love for us.
And because Jesus lived, died, and rose again,
We, too, will live eternally with Him,
For we are His.

The Riches of God

God's revelation of who He is
Prompts Him to display
His ever-increasing riches
And faithfulness each day.

We receive the riches
Of His unconditional love.
It's all about Him,
for God is love.

We receive the riches
Of His unmerited grace.
He freely gives us
What we do not deserve.

We receive the riches
Of His undeserved mercy.
He holds back and does not give us
What we actually deserve.

We indeed are chosen.
We're the ones who are so blessed.

With God's
Unconditional love,
His unmerited grace,
His undeserved mercy,
We are well equipped
To not only run
But win the race.

The True Rectifier

Trouble
Halts
Eventually.

Then the
Righteous and
Unbelievers
Experience

Returning
Everlasting
Christ
To
Intercede and
Fix
It and make
Everything
Right.

The Sanctuary

Enter into the sanctuary,
For protection from the storm.
There you will be
Secure, safe, and warm.

Go into the sanctuary,
Where you will find peace.
You will be calmed.
All worries will cease.

For into the sanctuary,
God's spirit unfolds.
It is in His presence
His glory you'll behold.

In the sanctuary,
Your spirit's lifted high.
God's love will surround you.
He's always nearby.

His Time

God comes when He wills,
Not when I will.
I'm just glad He comes,
Even still.

Not on cue, not on command,
Not always by prayer.
God comes when He wills.
He knows when to be there.

He is ever present
Yet doesn't always seem near.
God comes when He wills
To remove my doubt and fear.

God comes when He wills,
Not when I will.
I'm just glad He comes,
Even still.

God's Word

The Bible

The Bible is perfect,
        Inspired by God with a perfect plan,
        Written for every woman and man.
The Bible is timeless,
        An enduring book that our forefathers read
        That greatly affected their hearts and their heads.
The Bible is a light
        Shining to help us find our way,
        For we are often tempted to go astray.
The Bible is armor,
        Defending against Satan, trying to wear us out
        By always creating obstacles, opposition, and doubt.
The Bible is meat
        That nourishes the body and revives the soul,
        For its daily consumption makes us whole.
The Bible is an anchor
        That keeps us grounded during the storm,
        Keeping us safe and protected from harm.
The Bible is a map
        That leads, guides, and navigates our steps,
        The best book there is on self-help.

The Bible is history,
> Teaching us about the past
> But also the present and a future that will last.

The Bible is preparation
> For life and all that awaits,
> In order to be ready and never hesitate.

The Bible is a treasure
> Worth more than silver and gold.
> Its nuggets of truth enrich as they unfold.

The Bible is a best-seller
> Full of love, forgiveness, and grace.
> It can never be replaced.

The Bible is a must;
> Read it, study it, and from it learn
> To live a life that is steadfast and firm.

Newness

New things are new
Just for a while.
After much use,
They're pushed into a pile.

Things made by man
Will not last forever.
When they lose their function
They're replaced, discarded, or severed.

God's Word is different.
It's forever new.
What's contained within its pages
Will inform and inspire you.

The Bible is God's Word,
Written especially for us.
We must let it be our foundation.
It's like our living trust.

Trust what has been spoken,
Trust in who God is,
Trust in how He would have us live
If we want to be called His.

Power of the Word

God sent out His Word,
And fruit it did produce.
For all that it contains
Is filled with power and the truth.

Our joy is to share the Word
And leave the results to God.
He alone has the power.
He merits our highest regard.

The Word of God
Can revive the weary, convert the lost,
Direct the course of life,
And give hope to all.

It will accomplish
All He wants it to.
It will prosper wherever it's sent.
God desires that for me and you.

Isaiah 55:10–11

Life's Trials

A Blessed "No"

God pours out His blessings,
He even poured out His life,
So that I have an abundance
Of peace and joy, and no strife.

When God says no,
Never, or not yet,
It is often not the answer
I wanted to get.

So I should step back
And look at the broader scope,
One that is not distorted
But is filled with hope.

For God knows what is best.
Most often I cannot see.
When God says no, I must not fret—
He knows best. I let His will be.

As Is

"As Is" is the notice
On the purchase you might make.
It states that there are no guarantees
Just in case it breaks.

Hoping it works for a while,
You're willing to take the risk,
Getting some use out of it
Before it must be fixed.

We, too, can be like that:
Unreliable and used,
Thinking we know what is best,
Yet we're misguided and confused.

God is the only One
Who can take us "as is,"
Make us like brand-new,
And label us as His.

He places His seal of approval,
Guaranteeing eternal life,
Just like any loving Father,
He keeps us in His care, free from strife.

Be Encouraged

In learning to walk, you must first crawl.
And after knowing how, you still might fall.

In going to school, many tests you must take.
Some good and not-so-good grades you will make.

In order to drive, the wheel you must steer.
To maneuver in traffic, you overcome fear.

In taking your vows, all joy you expect,
But it's in your disagreements that you learn to respect.

In starting a new venture, you want the best,
But taking a loss might be your best test.

In picking the roses, you'll see the stems.
There are many thorns on each one of them.

In anything you do, there's potential for pain,
But don't let that fear make you refrain.

Everything worthwhile is worth working for.
Achieving what you want makes you the victor.

Don't let fear of failure get to your head.
Trust your instincts and pray instead.

Don't fall flat on your face.
Rely, then, on God's amazing grace.

God's guidance and His strength
Will reassure you and build your confidence.

Choices

Life is a constant series of choices.
In your mind, you hear many voices.

We can earn abundance and peace,
If our faith in God does not cease.

Live according to God's commands,
Disregarding what society demands.

Ultimately, you have to decide,
Thinking of consequences that will preside.

Disobedience will make you suffer,
Creating heartbreak and pain like no other.

When you confront a hard decision,
Seek God for His all-knowing provision.

Seek His wisdom, like He asked you to,
So you'll know exactly what to do.

Then trust completely in it.
To His will and guidance, just submit.

Spiritual abundance can be yours.
The right choice can open doors.

You will have blessings untold,
Day by day as they unfold.

Hope

With uncertainties, anxieties, and failures,
You seem to be losing ground,
They cause you to worry and distress,
And hope is nowhere to be found.

Ongoing trials and tribulations,
Tax your heart and trouble the mind,
You see no hope for the future,
The weights of life confine.

But no matter how desperate
Your circumstances seem, arrest them.
You can have hope right now,
If you place your hope in Him.

Hope is a strong and steady faith,
A sure confidence in the promise of God.
Hope is what you hold on to,
When adversities make life hard.

God has promised peace,
Eternal life, and joy.
You must not defer hope,
He wants abundant life for you to enjoy.

He keeps His promise,
Today, tomorrow, and forever.
He is faithful, you can trust Him,
His love will leave you never.

"Be of good courage,
He will strengthen your heart,
All of you who hope in the Lord."
From Psalm 31:24, do not depart. (NKJV)

Hurry up and Wait

Hurry up and wait
Is all that you can do
When something that you want
Doesn't come to you.

Hurry up and wait.
You know not when
What God has promised
He will send.

Hurry up and wait.
Just bide your time.
Realize that His timing
Is always the best time.

Hurry up and wait.
He's got the upper hand.
One day, more about his timing
We might understand.

Hurry up and wait.
Keep on trusting too.
God is faithful.
Believe what He can do.

Hurry up and wait.
Do not cease to pray.
Accept God's answer
As the best and only way.

Hurry up and wait.
God is waiting on your move.
It's in your time of waiting
He proves His love to you.

I Phone a Friend

If I need a recipe that I can't find,
I phone a friend who also knows my mind.

If I'm alone and my car won't start,
I phone a friend who comes with an open heart.

If I'm bothered by something I resent,
I phone a friend, sometimes just to vent.

If I'm elated by a great deal I found,
I phone a friend who's ready to go to town.

If my children apply my teachings they have used,
I phone a friend to share the good news.

When I miss someone and haven't called in a while,
I phone that friend and can hear her smile.

When I have sad news and I'm about to cry,
I phone a friend who with me will sigh.

But when something happens no earthly friend can aid,
I phone Jesus. His answer has already been made.

Recall

It happens to us all.
We have an occasional bout
Brought on by life's adversity,
By discouragement and doubt.

We say with our words
That we do trust God,
Yet we say with our lives
That it's just too hard.

We feel far removed,
Unsure of our next step.
We are tense and anxious.
We're in need of help.

We must then seek His presence,
Have a face-to-face.
He will calm our anxiety
And fill us with His grace.

He's promised to never leave us.
His words are always true.
We must dismiss the nagging doubt:
Recall, refresh, and begin anew.

We Need the Light

Jesus is the light of the world.
Even in these dark times,
This world that we live in
Has so increased in crime.

There is much hatred
And disregard of life,
Hopelessness, lovelessness,
Lives filled with strife.

Bad things are happening,
But evil's not in charge.
God's light still shines.
It is God who is in charge.

Lift up our eyes.
We need to see the light,
The light that You shine,
Even during the night.

We need Your light
So very much today.
Lead us back to You.
Help us find our way.

Obedience

Different Soils

Luke tells a parable
Of a man who sowed some grain.
It teaches a valued lesson
About the Word of God
And what we can gain.

Some of the seeds
Fell on the path.
They were stepped on and eaten by the birds,
Symbolizing how the devil steals from some,
And the Word is never heard.

Some of the seeds
Fell on rocky ground.
People gladly hear the Word at first,
But they do not stick around.

Some of the seeds
Fell among the thorn bushes,
Representing those whose worries and pleasures
Are fulfilled, choked by their own wishes.

But some of the seeds
Fell in good soil.
They are obedient and fruitful.
Satan, though he tries, cannot spoil.

As believers,
We must be deeply rooted,
Grounded only in Him,
To experience the joy
Of life more abundantly,
Given only by Him.

Following His Lead

I've been writing poems for some time.
There's something special about making words rhyme.

I often write instead of sending a card;
Making them right for that person is not hard.

I've been inspired from my morning read.
Often, that's where God plants a seed.

And sometimes when I'm asleep at night,
A new idea comes to light.

I then proceed to write it down,
To hear more of the rhyming sound.

My sister is my sounding board.
Through her encouragement, my writing soared.

She says it's a gift from above.
I know it's an expression of God's love.

I've never written so much before.
It seems as if God is opening a door.

For Him I will continue to write.
Praising God in poems is my delight.

I pray that my poems will lift someone,
Reminding them of all God has done.

Good Works

Salvation does not signal
The end of earthly work.
Indeed, it marks the start
Of work you cannot shirk.

As you grow in grace and learn,
Your faith too will grow strong.
It is by serving God
That good deeds come along.

Act on your beliefs,
For faith without works is dead.
Work gladly and dutifully.
Others will know
By Christ you are led.

Integrity

There are lasting rewards
That God bestows
On those who obey,
When one's integrity shows.

It is the sum of each right decision
And every honest word,
Each noble thought, each heartfelt prayer
That God has heard.

It is built upon the foundation
Of industry and working hard,
Generosity and sharing,
And humility that sets one apart.

It is a precious thing,
Quite difficult to build,
Yet always doing the right thing.
It is character you instill.

As believers in Christ,
We must seek to live
With discipline and honesty
And faith to reveal.

Be a person of integrity.
Be upright in words and deeds.
In your life you will be known
By the God you serve
and by the God who leads.

Power, Love, and Self-Discipline

Power, love, and self-discipline
Are what the Spirit gives
To all who are believers,
Showing us how to live.

His power enables us to work
To do what must be done
And do it in a way that
Fear and temptation are overcome.

His love enables us
To be a conduit of His grace,
Showing love to others
So they, too, can run this race.

His self-discipline fosters within us
An alert and sound mind,
So we may be about
Doing what is right and what is kind.

Life is not always easy.
He did not say that it would be,
But the Spirit's power, love, and self-discipline
Empowers us with liberty.

Serving

When Christ is at the center,
Your heart knows what to do:
You serve the One who saved you.
As He would have you do.

Help the ones
Who cannot help themselves.

Love the ones
Who do not love themselves.

Protect the ones
Who cannot shield themselves.

Care for the ones
Who can't care for themselves.

You then will be obedient
To 1 Peter 5:2.
You are admonished
To shepherd the flock of God,
Which is among you.

Sow a Seed

Interestingly enough,
Simply sow a seed
To get what you want.
Give away what you need.

The seed takes root
And begins to grow
When God's love
To others you show.

Sit with the lonely
Or feed the hungry,
Encourage the sad,
Sharing experiences that you've had.

Visit those who are ill;
Show you care how they feel.
Assist wherever you can
With your helping hands.

Babysit the neighbor's kids,
Take the elderly to the store,
Volunteer to clean a house.
Opportunities are endless, so many more.

Prepare a meal,
Ease someone's loss or pain.
It's when you help and serve
That you benefit and gain.

When you sacrifice
To help someone else,
You are sowing a seed
And growing yourself.

But that's how God works:
When you become His hands and feet
By fulfilling the needs of others,
Then your own needs He meets.

Sow and Reap

"You reap what you sow"
Is an often-quoted truth.
You harvest what you plant,
And its results you produce.

If you do evil,
Expect it in return.
Just as you have burned others,
One day you will burn.

If you do good,
Expect it in return.
Just as you have shown favor,
Favor you will earn.

This very simple fact
Is easy for you to see:
Beware of what you plant,
For that is what will be.

Step up to the Plate

God created you for a reason.
It is revealed in due season,
His purpose and His plan,
Since time began.

He has important work for you to do.
The next step is up to you.
He waits patiently for you to do it.
Your heart must be committed to it.

Love and help someone in pain.
Know your labor will not be in vain.
Share the good news with someone;
Tell them about the saving work of God's Son.

Not only must we take a stand
For our hurting and deprived land,
We must also step up to the plate.
Fulfill God's purpose before it's too late.

Teach the Children

They need to know.
Children are to be taught, as God commands,
All about Him so they understand.

They need to know
Our God from the past
Will give us a life that will forever last.

They need to know
His commandments and laws
And how obedience eases our flaws.

They need to know
The things God dislikes
And what is pleasing in His sight.

They need to know
How to grow in the knowledge of Him
And learn how much He loves them.

They need to know
Of the many promises He makes
And know that none of them will He ever break.

They need to know
Of God's mercy, love, and grace,
And how much life is like a race.

They need to know
How God loves and sustains
And how His presence with us remains

We need to know
It's up to us to love, discipline, and teach,
If God's children we want to reach.

We need to know
They hear what we say in our talk
And they see what we do in our walk.

We need to know
Our children will grow and be well-fed
If by God's Word they have been led.

Peace

Peace

Peace is harmony and accord,
In cordial relations with others and the Lord.
Sourced in Christ and the Holy Spirit,
Christians are admonished to pursue it.

We need to be at peace with the past.
Mistakes result from acting too fast.
From those experiences we did learn
To take time to pray and to discern.

With the present, we must be content,
Being cautious of how our time is spent.
Striving to do the best we can,
Doing what's right and taking a stand.

With the future, we must be sure
That our place in heaven is secure,
Knowing that all is in His hands.
From the beginning, that was His plan.

Claim the peace that only God can give.
It's offered freely as we live.
Feel the spiritual abundance of peace,
For the love of God will never cease.

Peace Only Comes

When we
Position
Everything
Around
Christ's
Example.

Sweet Peace

When into our lives, tragedies are thrust,
Absolute and undoubting trust
In the love of God is a must.

For only God knows the why.
Trust and accept
His sovereignty on high.

It is by His will
That He allowed it to be,
Yet through our eyes,
We simply cannot see.

God can turn things around
For His glory and for our gain;
If we only trust in Him,
Sweet peace we can attain.

"For whatsoever is born of God
Overcometh the world.
And this is the victory that
Overcometh the world,
Even our faith."
So 1 John 5:4 states.

People in the Bible

Apostle Paul

Saul witnessed the stoning of Stephen
And persecuted Christian believers, even.

On the Damascus road, God blinded his eyes,
But at the same time, they were opened.

From that point on, his life changed:
New focus, new purpose, he was even renamed.
Paul was the first to preach to non-Jews,
Traveling thousands of miles to spread the good news.

A powerful witness, telling what God had done.
Many were converted, many souls were won.

Paul suffered much after he was saved.
He did not grumble, nor did he complain.
He continued to preach in Jesus's name.

In bonds, stoned and arrested,
He was also shipwrecked and exiled.
Patiently enduring, still encouraging,
Still preaching all the while.

The Bible contains many letters he wrote.
They still apply today; many verses we quote.

Apostle Paul is one to admire
For his faith that never did tire.

He fought a good fight.
He finished his course.
He kept the faith.
For his crown of righteousness,
He did wait.

Fearless Zephaniah

Blessings, prosperity, and safety
Are what God's promises recall
To Israel if they obeyed
His commands and His laws.

Hardship, defeat, and curses,
On the other hand,
Are what God promised
For disobeying His commands.

The city, however, became polluted
With false religion, idolatry, and evil things,
Mistreatment of the poor and widows,
Led by evil leaders and kings.

God always sent prophets
To warn and to remind
Of the coming judgment,
For the promises they left behind.

With no immediate consequences,
They continued with no fear,
With no thought of tomorrow
And judgment being near.

Israel mocked the messengers
And despised their words,
Misusing the prophets,
Ignoring all they heard.

With no moral compass,
By pagans they were led,
Forsaking the truth
And trusting self instead.

The judgment of neighboring countries
Should have served them well.
For God's laws they would ignore,
But they could not dispel.

It was forty years before
Zephaniah's words came true.
God was patient in His judgment
As their disobedience grew.

Israel was foolish and preposterous
To think their way was best.
For the life God had required of them
Was for their highest good
And would make them truly blessed.

Disobedience has consequences.
We can order our lives instead,
Not for judgment
But for the blessings God so loves to serve.

Joseph and His Brothers

Joseph's brothers hated his coat and his dreams.
Put him in a pit and sell him as a slave, they schemed.

He was put in charge of Potiphar's house,
But imprisoned for lies from his spouse.

There he interpreted Pharaoh's dream.
He wisely explained what it could mean.

From there he would lead all Egypt land.
Seven years of plenty and seven of famine began.

Joseph's father sent the brothers there for grain,
Not knowing this leader and Joseph were one and the same.

Joseph gave orders for them to return.
It was then his identity they would learn.

Joseph reassured his brothers, who understood
What they meant for evil, God meant for good.

Joseph and Mary Flee to Egypt

Wicked King Herod was deeply disturbed
When he heard of the wise men's word.
He called to meet the leaders of the Jews
To get the details of this news.

Where was this Messiah supposed to be
That these men came so very far to see?
In Bethlehem is what Herod was told;
It was then his plan would unfold.

Herod sent word for the wise men to return;
Their specific whereabouts he must learn.
"When you find the baby, come back to me,
So that I may worship him too, you see."

The wise men followed the star once more.
They found the baby Jesus on the manger floor.
Their hearts were filled with so much joy
When they saw the newborn baby boy.

They bowed down and worshipped him.
Gold, frankincense, and myrrh were gifts from them.
They did not return to Herod that day,
For God had warned them to go another way.

An angel appeared to Joseph in a dream that night:
"You must leave Bethlehem; prepare for flight.
Get up at once and leave this place
So Herod cannot find even a trace.

"Flee to Egypt with Mary and the baby.
Stay there awhile, for your own safety.
King Herod will try to kill the child,
This baby Jesus, so holy and mild."

Joseph and family left that night.
Herod was furious yet full of fright.
He looked for them, poor Herod, he tried,
But they stayed in Egypt until he died.

The prophet's prediction had begun:
"I have called from Egypt, my Son."
Nothing could ever change our Savior's plan.
Jesus, Son of God, the Son of Man.

King David

He was a shepherd, a giant-slayer,
And a poet, among other things.
He was handpicked by God
To become the next king.

God anointed him king
And rescued him from Saul.
He gave him wives and a kingdom.
David had it all.

He became callous
In his adulterous sin.
The only way to cover it
Was to murder and sin again.

God sent Nathan,
Who related his wrong
And told how he disobeyed
And disgraced the throne.

David acknowledged his sin,
And the relationship he broke.
God forgave him,
But consequences He evoked.

David became diligent
And faithful in everything.
He became greatest
Of all Israel's kings.

He was a man
After God's own heart.
His love, mercy, and faithfulness
To David He did impart.

David had the joy
Of his salvation restored
And once again experienced
The presence and the power
Of the Holy Spirit that he adored.

King Solomon

Obey the laws of God
And follow all His ways.
Keep the laws of Moses
To prosper all your days.

This is the charge King David
Gave to Solomon, his son:
To fulfill the promise
That God gave to him alone.

The Lord appeared to Solomon
In a dream one night
And told him to ask for what he wanted,
And it would be given outright.

Solomon asked for wisdom
So that he could govern well,
To know the difference between right and wrong
For the high position he held.

God gave Solomon wisdom,
But it was up to him to apply
In governing the nation and his life
That he needed to supply.

He went against his father's words,
Disobeying God's commands.
This wisest man who ever lived
Let success and contentment slip through his hands.

There were drastic repercussions
Because of Solomon's sin.
It stands in stark contrast to God's favor
That He now must rescind.

It was only late in life
That Solomon learned to repent,
Being truly sorry
For how his life was spent.

From this, we can also learn
When we make mistakes—and we will.
Repent to God immediately and proceed.
He forgives and loves you still.

Mrs. Job

She too, like her husband,
Lost all she ever had:
Her children, her servants, and her wealth.
These dreadful losses made her very sad.

She watched her husband suffer
With sores from head to toe.
Her doubt and disbelief
Made her blame God all the more.

Troubles overwhelmed her.
She decided that God did not care.
She succumbed to hopelessness;
For her, God was not there.

She advised poor Job
To curse God and die.
She felt betrayed and hurt
And couldn't understand why.

Though Job suffered much,
For reasons he didn't understand,
His faith in God remained.
And He restored Job with children, wealth, and land.

I wonder about Mrs. Job
And if she truly learned
That if God is your foundation,
Your faith won't waver and will be stern.

Peter's Focus

Jesus told the disciples
To get into the boat
And go to the other side
Of the lake.

Jesus sent the people away
To go by himself and pray.
This was something that He did
Several times a day.

The wind was blowing hard,
Tossing the boat about.
As Jesus walked on water,
The disciples were filled with doubt.

They were terrified
And screamed out loud with fear.
Jesus calmly said, "Have courage,
It is I," as He drew near.

Peter courageously spoke:
"Lord, if it is really You,
Order me to come out
On the water there with You."

Peter was quite wise
To wait for Jesus to say, "Come."
He exited the boat with confidence,
Going to the Son.

As soon as Peter got out
And walked upon the water,
He noticed the strong wind
And did hesitate and falter.

Peter forgot who was there,
Keeping him afloat.
And he started doubting again,
The same fear he had within the boat.

He was afraid
Of what he could not see.
So he cried out,
"Save me, Lord." This was his urgent plea.

At once, Jesus reached out
And grabbed ahold of him,
Rebuking Peter of his doubts
And his faith that had dimmed.

When we keep our eyes on Jesus
And not upon the storm,
He will surely save us
And protect us from all harm.

We must continue on in faith,
Though the testing may be hard.
And we too, like the disciples,
Will know He truly is the Son of God.

The Prodigal Son

Scripture relates the parable
Of a father and younger son
Who asked for his inheritance
Before his father was gone.

His father, gracious and generous,
Granted him his request.
The son took his new fortune
And started on his quest.

With his indulgent lifestyle,
It was not very long;
From all the riotous living
All his wealth was soon gone.

This young man took a job
In order to survive.
He fed and fattened the pigs,
Starving, trying to stay alive.

He came to his senses and said,
"To home I will go back,"
Not knowing exactly
How his father would react.

The father had been watching
For his son each day.
When he saw him returning,
He ran and met him on the way.

His father gladly restored him
With a celebration and food to eat.
It was the position he once enjoyed
But now with robe, ring, and sandals for his feet.

Everything the son hoped for,
He discovered back at home:
Love, assurance, and mercy
Were there all along.

This parable portrays our Father,
Who wants us to return
To a relationship with Him,
For blessings, love, and joy
That we will soon learn.

The Rich Young Ruler

The rich young ruler
Asked what he had to do
To inherit eternal life.
He perceived himself as good,
But his assurance
He was lacking.

He was told to sell it all
And give it to the poor
To gain a treasure in heaven,
The blessing he desired.

He went away feeling sad,
Although he had not lost
Any riches that he held.
He valued all his riches.
They made him feel secure.

All thoughts of eternal life—
Now he was not so sure.
Sadly, he did not believe
What God supplies
Is far greater than
Anything else in our lives.

The Servant Who Lacked

Those who have, get more.
Those with little, lose that.
So goes the parable of Luke 19
About the servant who lacked.

He lacked the king's interest.
He lacked his trust.
He lacked loyalty,
Avoiding what he must.

His loyalty was to himself.
He did not use his gifts.
Everything he had
Was for his own benefit.

He gained nothing
And failed to understand.
He lost the little he held
In his closefisted hand.

The other servants
Used their gifts and reported gain;
They were given even more,
Much more they retained.

Watch, listen, and follow
Are your challenges, then;
What God calls you to do,
He enables you to attend.

The Woman With Healing Faith

For twelve long years, this woman did bleed.
No earthly doctor could meet her need.

When all of her money was spent and gone,
She was helpless and all alone.

Then she heard about Jesus among the crowd
That was so congested and packed and loud.

She thought to herself, *If I could only touch
the cloak of the Lord; it can do so much.*

As soon as she did, she could tell
That she was made instantly well.

Jesus asked who had touched his clothes.
His disciples answered, "Who could know?"

But Jesus looked around to see
The woman, who came and knelt at his feet.

"It was your faith," Jesus revealed.
"Go in peace; you have been healed."

Praise

Christmas 1981

I never shall forget
The best Christmas of all;
The one of 1981
Is the easiest to recall.

He had been laid off
From his full-time job;
Trying to make it on my pay
Was becoming hard.

On Thanksgiving weekend,
Our family roller-skated;
After being pushed and falling,
My shoulder separated.

Hospitalized for nine days,
I was in a lot of pain.
I worried, though, about Christmas
And our financial strain.

Upon returning home,
I found we had a tree;
It was already decorated
And there were gifts for our kids, all three.

Every day thereafter,
Money and gifts we received;
To our surprise, it was far more
Than we would need.

I was so very grateful
And was brought to tears.
Our wallets, fridge, and cabinets
Were filled despite my fears.

I regret my worry
About how we would survive,
Not realizing God would take care
And how He would provide.

God has shown us over and over,
When in difficult times.
I have no need to worry.
He cares for me and mine.

Gift of Faith

It is by grace that you've been saved,
Through faith, and not of yourselves.
It is the gift of God.
Use it; don't put it on a shelf.

You cannot receive the gift by works,
So that none can boast.
Hence, when you receive this gift,
Thank the Giver who loves you most.

Faith that believes it
Is the faith that prays
To recognize His power
And understand His ways.

We live by faith
And not by sight,
Belief and confidence
That God has all might.

The reason for our faith
Is not so our wants are filled,
But to submit to a Holy God
For our will to align with His.

God's Got My Back

God's got my back,
My front, my all around.
Wherever I am,
His presence can be found.

What have I to fear?
What have I to dread?
Wherever I go,
God has gone ahead.

Whenever problems arise,
Satan brings on his dare.
Whatever I must do,
God is always there.

Yes, God's got me covered.
I know He's got my back.
Whenever I have fallen,
He puts me back on track.

God has me in His care.
He's looking out for me.
Nothing can happen
That God does not see.

It's good to be protected
And to be secure.
Come what may,
I know I can endure.

I Saw Daddy

"Please don't let me blow it as a dad"
Had to be the prayer my daddy had.

For I saw in him a special love
That comes only from favor above.

I saw the many sacrifices that Daddy always made
So that his family's debts were always paid.

I saw Daddy work real hard.
He was industrious, talented, and so very smart.

I saw Daddy give all his pay.
He always knew God would make a way.

I saw Daddy help those in need,
Be it one or an entire family to feed.

I saw Daddy's contagious smile,
Even though he had his own trials.

The short life that Daddy lived
Was productive, blessed, and God-filled.

He was the father God called him to be.
He lived his life for his children to see.

"Please don't let me blow it as a dad"
Had to be the prayer my daddy had.

P is for Praise

Thank You, Lord, for Your **plan**
For which Your Son did die,
So that I may live
In heaven on high.

Thank You, Lord, for Your **power.**
Your strength amazes me.
You speak a word
And determine what will be.

Thank You for the **peace**
That only You can give.
It gets me through the day
As You would have me live.

Thank You for **provisions**
That supply my needs each day.
Even when I'm uncertain,
You always make a way.

Thank You for Your **patience**
And not giving up on me
When I do and say things
That are not pleasing to Thee.

Thank You for Your **protection**
In times of hurt and harm.
You encircle and protect me
In Your loving arms.

Thank You for Your **promises**
Found in Your Holy Book.
They give me so much hope
Each time that I look.

Thank You for Your **presence,**
For You are always there.
Where I've been or where I go,
You are everywhere.

Thank You for **prayers**
Because You hear what I say.
They help me face tomorrow
And make everything okay.

P is for **praise.**
You are so worthy, Lord.
I praise You for who I am and what I can do,
Based on love and blessings that come from You.

Therefore, through Him let us continually offer up to God a sacrifice of praise, that is, the fruit of our lips that confess His name.
—Hebrews 13:15 (ISV)

Treasured

In God's Holy Word,
Specifically, Deuteronomy 14:2,
To be His treasured possession,
The Lord has chosen you.

The world came into existence,
By the words that God spoke.
All belongs to Him,
Yet He values you the most.

That makes you special,
More precious than any gold.
Of all of His creations,
It is you He beholds.

That should come as no surprise;
His love, it is quite clear.
For you, He gave His only begotten,
Whom He loved so dear.

To be chosen by God,
Is an honor and blessing, too.
To Him, you are so prized;
To Him, you must be true.

What More Can I Do?

Without You, Lord, life could never be.
From sin and fear, You set me free.
Thanking You, Lord, is not enough.
What more can I do? I love You so much.

Thank You, Lord, for the past.
Your sacrifice will forever last.
Your Son died to save me from sin,
To give me hope and peace within.

Thank You, Lord, for the time right now.
Your mercies flow each day somehow.
You hear all the prayers I pray to You.
You supply my needs and protect me too.

Thank You, Lord, for tomorrow.
Because of You, I have no sorrow.
You've prepared a place for me.
I'll be with You eternally.

What more can I do to live my life for You?
What more can I say to show others the way?

I can love as You loved
And serve as You served.
I can give as You gave
And pray as You prayed.
I can let others see You in me.
That would be my way
Of praising Thee.

Prayer

Bow the Knee

Every knee shall bow,
And every tongue must confess,
Recognizing the Lord and Savior
Whom all will address.

But until He returns
For all who believe,
Go to Him in prayer,
His presence to receive.

Humbly seek His face
With all your heart.
Get to know Him better,
For His will to impart.

Be meek and reverent as you pray.
Meet Him on bended knee.
For honor, glory, and praise
Are due Him for all to see.

Meeting Him

"For God alone my soul waits in silence."
So says Psalm 62:5.
When I meet God in prayer,
I benefit and thrive.

I am enveloped
By His welcoming, open arms.

I am surrounded
By His healing, radiant light.

I am enfolded
By His holy presence.

I am comforted
By His Holy Spirit.

I am renewed completely:
Mind, body, and soul.

For the peace, joy, and love
I get
When I meet God in prayer.

My Alone Time

If I want God to speak to me,
It is I who must prepare, not He.

I must drown out all the noise,
So my heart and mind are poised.

I must get quiet and be still,
If God's presence I want to feel.

If I need that still, quiet voice,
Undivided attention must be my choice.

I give Him mind, body, and soul,
So that His love I can behold.

The God who spoke the world into being
Is the same Lord I fixate on seeing.

I am blessed
With love, fellowship, and grace
In my alone time
When I seek His face.

Pray

When do I pray?
        Morning, night, and in between.
        God's presence I always see.

How do I pray?
        Standing, sitting, or on bended knee.
        God is everywhere I need Him to be.

Where do I pray?
        At home, at church, at work, or at play.
        God acknowledges me in every way.

For whom do I pray?
        For myself, my family, and all across the world.
        God hears every man, woman, boy, and girl.

For what do I pray?
        For things I can do and those I can't.
        In every circumstance, He can work it out.

Why do I pray?
        Praying to God is a believer's must.
        For God wants a relationship with us.

What happens if I don't pray?
        I am choosing to disobey
        And missing blessings sent my way.

Let us pray before, after, and at all times.
Let prayers avail in your life and mine.

Pray to God

If your faith is weak,
Pray to God.
He will answer
And override your unbelief.

If your faith is the kind
To which God responds,
Then you are using your gift.
It's how He wants it done.

Don't allow challenges
To interrupt your faith.
It is God who allows them
To strengthen and motivate.

Let us then accept this gift
And not let it go to waste.
Know we have the power
To run this Christian race.

Watch and Pray

Jesus tells us in His word,
To watch and to pray.
We can overcome temptation,
If these words we would obey.

Watch and pray.
Satan is evil, always on the prowl,
Constantly looking for
Someone he can devour.

You are in God's hands,
You are His concern.
Watch and pray,
So that Satan's temptation,
You can easily discern.

God will not let you be tempted,
Beyond what you can bear.
Watch and pray,
God will be with you,
He will be there.

Purpose

Before and After

Before Christ in my life		After Christ in my life
I was lost in sin	now	Forgiveness is within.
It was all about me	now	I think only of Thee.
I knew not Your Word	now	Your Word is heard.
I lived in worry and fear	now	Your presence is near.
Confusion was all around	now	Peace and joy abound.
Darkness was all right	now	I see the light.
I accepted defeat	now	My joy is complete.
I was led by selfish desires	now	I'm led by what Christ requires.
I often had the blues	now	I share the good news.
I felt misery and strife	now	I have abundant life.
I had frustration and emptiness	now	I have mercy and goodness.
I felt disconnected	now	I am protected.
I was tempted to disobey	now	I live Your way.
I trusted my emotions	now	I trust Your devotion.
I needed to change my ways	now	I give You all the praise.

Get It

Get what you need
With a new life in Christ.

Get the many benefits
That come from His sacrifice.

Get forgiveness
And a fresh new start.

Get reassurance
From peace and joy in your heart.

Get a new perspective
That you are loved.

Get appreciation
Of His many blessings from above.

Get directives and directions,
Which keep you from going astray.

Get all that you need
With Christ, who is the only way.

Spiritual Maturity

As a believer, you must never cease to grow,
If more of God's love you want to know.

You must study His Word and obey His command,
Be in His will and then understand.

Ask for direction to make the right choice.
Follow His lead and hear His voice.

Ask for perspective to see His view.
Align your will with His to know what to do.

Ask for wisdom with more insight.
Use His knowledge to shed more light.

Ask for courage to do what must be done.
Stand for right, even if you're the only one.

Spiritual maturity is a lifelong journey.
Continue to grow.
God will bless your learning.

Yet to Come

God said in His Word,
In this world in which we live,
That we will have tribulations.
They are for real.

But He also prepared us,
So that we wouldn't fret,
And so that we would know
We haven't seen the best, not yet.

In John 16:33,
We're told to be of good cheer.
This world He has overcome.
We have no need to fear.

That was His plan,
Before time began.
He prepared a place for us,
In heaven's land.

That's why I love His Word,
For all the promises of hope.
We need His reassurance,
　So we do not lose hope.

We haven't seen the best,
　Even when all is well.
Because when we finally meet Him,
　All will be absolutely swell.

The problems of the present
　Will not endure.
But of the promise of the future,
　Of heaven, I am sure.

Temptations

The Devil

"Devil" and "devious"
Both start the same.
Being true to his character,
"Devious" describes his name.

"Devil" and "evil"
Both end the same.
What is interesting
Is that "evil" describes his game.

"Devil" and "revile":
Both middle parts are the same.
And as you would surmise,
They both reference shame.

"Devil" and "devour"
Also start the same.
It is what he does,
But he never takes the blame.

The devil is a demon
Who is good at his evil game.
He aims to destroy,
Discredit, destruct, corrupt, and defame.

These letters have more in common
Than just the words they spell.
They all signify wickedness
And describe Satan very well.

Lay Them Aside

Lay aside the weight and sins that ensnare,
For Satan will trap you unaware.
You work hard and try to succeed.
You often earn much more than you need.

Before long, Satan tries to distract,
Convincing you that you still lack.
The material possessions you accumulate
Don't bring happiness, just feelings of hate.

These heavy weights change your direction,
Causing regrets and much reflection.
You dislike the person you've become.
You're confused, misguided, and undone.

Discard whatever challenges you:
Sins, bad habits, and overworking too.
Set your mind with determination
To rid yourself of weighted accumulation.

God wants your full attention.
He wants it all, with no dissention.
He wants it right now, today.
Don't let anything or anyone get in your way.

On Guard

They are my thoughts,
And so it's up to me
To guard what I think
About what should or shouldn't be.

There are regrets from the past,
Frustrations of today;
Uncertainties about tomorrow
Can cloud my vision and get in the way.

I then must guard my thoughts,
Rein them in and take their power,
Lest they discourage me and rob me of hope.
They make me cold and dour.

I must remember who I am,
That I've been bought with a price.
I redirect my thoughts to Him,
Without thinking twice.

God's ultimate wisdom
And His amazing grace
Help me refocus and endure
To run life's race.

God's love and His power
Are where my thoughts return
For the comfort, strength,
Patience, and perspective
I have already learned.

Seasons of Attack

Seasons of attack are inevitable.
They come to us all.
What we do determines our fate.
We can win or surely fall.

First and foremost,
Recall what God's Word states:
This spiritual battle is not ours.
It's His; make no mistake.

However, there is a role
That we must play:
Read the Bible, memorize verses,
And most importantly, we must pray.

Increase your wisdom, faith, and strength
Until the battle's done.
This kind of preparation
Will decide your life's outcome.

In doing so, you become
Spiritually strong and mentally fit.
You will be victorious,
And all the glory then, God will get.

Seeking Snails

About a snail-seeking crane
A legend has been told,
And about a beautiful swan
For one's eyes to behold.

She told the crane about heaven,
Of its grandeur and splendor,
With hosts of saints and angels,
Full of awe and wonder.

The eternal city
Has golden streets,
Walls and gates of precious stones,
And trees with healing leaves.

After the swan spoke, the crane's
Interest seemed to pale,
When he asked about heaven
And if there were snails.

He and many others
Turn their backs on God
And will miss out on heaven
For snails held in high regard.

Side Step of Deception

This side step of deception
Takes the long way around,
For dishonesty and deception
Keep you emotionally bound.

The side step of deception
Takes you where you shouldn't go.
You think it is the easiest,
But it's the hardest, you should know.

The idea of deception
Is part of Satan's scheme
To sway the way you think,
To make things unlike what they seem.

You are dishonest and you lie.
One lie leads to another.
You cannot face the truth.
Your deeds you try to cover.

Be honest with yourself.
Opt to not deceive.
The truth is always best,
For the peace of mine received.

You'll reach your destination
Much sooner than you thought.
You won't ever be sidetracked
If honesty is always sought.

Sin

Sin is sin.
Call it what you may.
It's disobeying God,
Doing things your own way.

God gave you free will
To do as you choose.
You put yourself in harm's way.
With sin, there's much to lose.

In this world we live,
The sin business thrives.
It comes in all shapes and sizes,
With potential to destroy our lives.

To the ever tempting distractions,
We should never yield.
For the consequences we suffer,
They are very real.

We must turn away from sin.
Jesus paid the price.
It was through His death and
His life-saving sacrifice.

Weeds

Weeds are unwanted,
As we all know.
The more we try to rid them,
The higher they seem to grow.

They grow and sprout
At a very fierce rate,
Making it almost impossible
To completely eliminate.

It seems that our efforts
Never will end.
Various preventative measures
Cannot rescind.

Weeds can be likened
To the sins in our lives:
They creep up on us,
They control and they thrive.

They must be treated
And plucked out
Before the destruction
They bring about.

Tend to them soon
Or they'll get out of hand.
When left unattended,
They are in command.

With nasty hidden sins,
There is much work to do.
They must be destroyed
Or they will destroy you.

Acknowledgments

I would like to acknowledge and thank those who played a role in writing my first book. Friends and family listened and encouraged me to publish it. Dear friends Arlene Banfield and LaRoyce Beatty took their time to edit these poems and offer suggestions. Dr. Marcus Blakemore offered his expertise in providing publication options. And I would like to thank Bill, my husband, for his patience, understanding, love, and support.

About the Author

Avar Hurd James was born in 1945 in Memphis, Tennessee.

She earned her BA from LeMoyne Owen College, her master's from the University of Memphis, and her EdS from Lincoln Memorial University in Harrogate, Tennessee. She taught in Memphis City Schools and retired from Alcoa City Schools in Alcoa, Tennessee. She also served as an educational consultant with the Tennessee Department of Education.

She has been actively involved with Bible Study Fellowship and Alpha Kappa Alpha Sorority, Inc. She is a deaconess at Mt. Calvary Baptist Church in Knoxville, Tennessee.

Avar and her husband reside in Maryville, Tennessee, and are the parents of Will, Chris, and Ashley, and the grandparents of Ashton, Gabi, Camille, and Brooklyn.

This is her first book.

Made in the USA
Coppell, TX
09 February 2022